A Home on the Savanna

By Susan Labella

Children's Press®
A Division of Scholastic Inc.
New York Toronto London Auckland Sydney
Mexico City New Delhi Hong Kong
Danbury, Connecticut

These content vocabulary word builders are for grades 1–2.
Subject Consultant: Susan Woodward, Professor of Geography, Radford University, Radford, Virginia

Reading Consultant: Cecilia Minden-Cupp, PhD, Former Director of the Language and Literacy Program, Harvard Graduate School of Education, Cambridge, Massachusetts

Photographs © 2007: Corbis Images: 23 bottom right (Frank Krahmer/zefa), 20 top (Paul A. Souders); Dembinsky Photo Assoc.: 23 top left (Mike Barlow), 20 bottom (Wendy Dennis), 23 top right (Adam Jones), 1, 5 bottom left, 9 (Fritz Polking), 4 bottom left, 19, 21 top (Anup Shah), 23 bottom left (Mark J. Thomas), cover right inset, 5 top right, 16 (Martin Withers); Minden Pictures: 13 (Gerry Ellis/Globio), cover left inset, back cover, 5 top left, 5 bottom right, 8, 12 (Mitsuaki Iwago), 21 bottom (Frans Lanting), cover background (Konrad Wothe), 4 top right, 17 (Shin Yoshino); Nature Picture Library Ltd./Peter Blackwell: 2, 7; Peter Arnold Inc./Martin Harvey: 11; Photo Researchers, NY/Michel & Christine Denis-Huot: cover center inset, 4 bottom right, 15.

Book Design: Simonsays Design!
Book Production: The Design Lab

Library of Congress Cataloging-in-Publication Data

Labella, Susan, 1948–
   A home on the savanna / by Susan Labella.
      p. cm. — (Scholastic news nonfiction readers)
   Includes index.
   ISBN-10: 0-516-25348-4
   ISBN-13: 978-0-516-25348-0
   1. Savanna ecology—Juvenile literature. I. Title. II. Series.
   QH541.5.P7L33 2006
   577.4'8—dc22   2006002883

1 2 3 4 5 6 7 8 9 10 R 16 15 14 13 12 11 10 09 08 07

CONTENTS

WORD HUNT

Look for these words as you read. They will be in **bold**.

gazelles
(guh-**zelz**)

lion
(**lye**-uhn)

mammals
(**mah**-muhlz)

habitat
(**hab**-uh-tat)

herds
(**hurdz**)

savanna
(suh-**vah**-nuh)

tusks
(**tuhsks**)

What Is This Place?

Grasses cover the land. There aren't many trees.

Sometimes the land seems all brown. Other times, it's completely green.

You hear a **lion** roar. You see an elephant stomp by.

Where are we?

**Lions are fierce hunters.
They often hunt in groups.**

We're on a **savanna** in Africa!

A savanna is a type of **habitat**. A habitat is where a plant or animal usually lives.

Savannas are grassy plains.

habitat

Savannas cover nearly half of Africa.

A savanna does not get enough rain for many trees to grow. But savannas get more rain than deserts.

The savanna has only two seasons. One is the wet season. The other is the dry season.

The savanna is warm most of the year.

Water is hard to find during the dry season.

Elephants use their tusks to dig for water underground. The holes they dig are called elephant wells. **Tusks** are long, curved teeth.

tusk

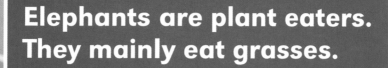

Elephants are plant eaters. They mainly eat grasses.

There is plenty of water for plants and animals during the wet season.

The grass turns green and grows fast.

Many baby **mammals** are born at this time.

Mammals, such as leopards, live on the savanna.

Animals of all sizes live on the savanna. Lizards, mice, and termites live there. So do lions, giraffes, and baboons.

Animals such as zebras and **gazelles** live in big groups, or **herds**.

herd

Gazelles are small, fast antelopes.

The savanna is an exciting place to explore! Pack some water and head through the grasses. You'll meet this giraffe and other amazing animals that live in this habitat!

A DAY IN THE LIFE OF A ZEBRA

How does a zebra spend most of its time? A zebra grazes.

What does a zebra eat? A zebra eats grasses.

What are a zebra's enemies? Lions, leopards, and hyenas are a zebra's enemies.

Does a zebra have a special survival trick? A zebra lives in a herd. Other animals in the herd are always on the lookout for danger. A zebra is also able to run at high speeds.

YOUR NEW WORDS

gazelles (guh-**zelz**) small, fast antelopes that live in Africa and Asia

habitat (**hab**-uh-tat) the place where a plant or animal usually lives

herds (**hurdz**) groups of the same kinds of animals

lion (**lye**-uhn) a large, light brown wildcat that lives in Asia and Africa

mammals (**mah**-muhlz) animals that are usually covered with hair and that produce milk to feed their young

savanna (suh-**vah**-nuh) a flat, treeless grassland found in hot parts of the world

tusks (**tuhsks**) long, curved teeth

OTHER ANIMALS THAT LIVE ON THE SAVANNA

cheetahs

ostriches

rhinoceroses

wildebeests

23

INDEX

FIND OUT MORE
Book:
Dunphy, Madeleine, and Tom Leonard (illustrator). *Here Is the African Savanna.* New York: Hyperion Books for Children, 1999.

Website:
Blue Planet Biomes: The Savanna
http://www.blueplanetbiomes.org/savanna.htm

MEET THE AUTHOR:
Susan Labella is a former teacher and editor. She is currently a freelance writer and has written other books for Scholastic Library Publishing.